A New Beginning

Subhadra Sen Gupta

Om Books International

After eighteen days, the terrible battle at Kurukshetra came to an end. Many of the greatest kings and warriors, including Bhishma, Dronacharya and Karna were dead. With the death of Duryodhana at Bhima's hands, the Kaurava family had lost all the sons of Gandhari and Dhritarashtra.

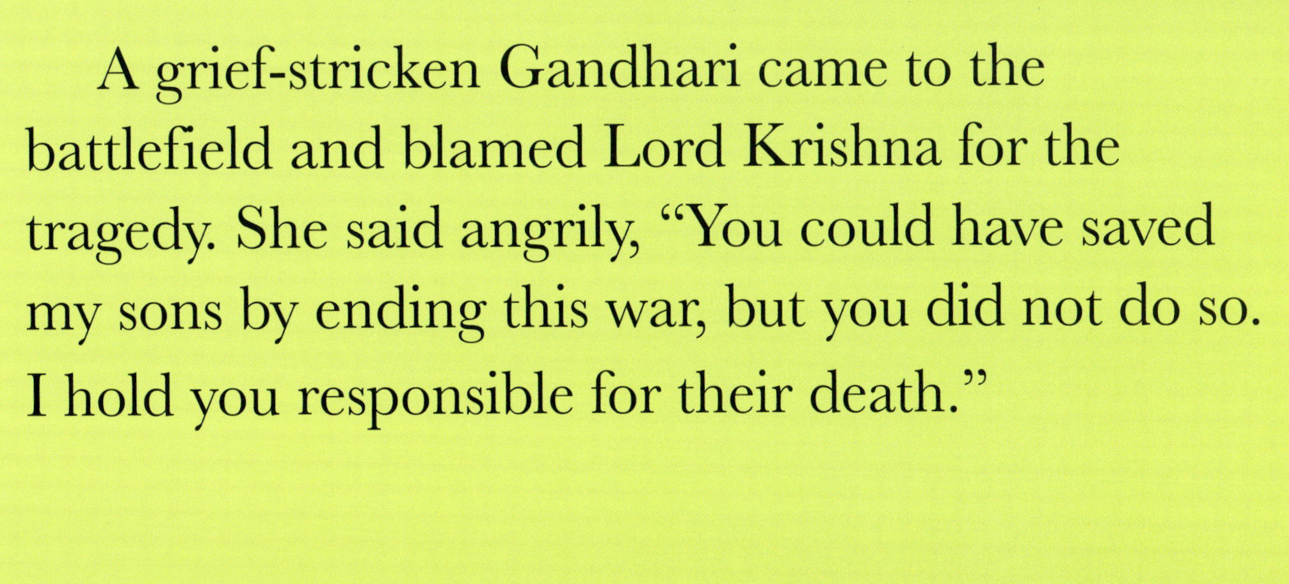

A grief-stricken Gandhari came to the battlefield and blamed Lord Krishna for the tragedy. She said angrily, "You could have saved my sons by ending this war, but you did not do so. I hold you responsible for their death."

Then she cursed Lord Krishna, "Just as I have watched all my sons die, one day you will also see all your sons and grandsons die before you. And you will not be able to do anything to stop it. You will then die all alone!"

Thirty-six years later, Gandhari's terrible curse came true when the men of Lord Krishna's clan, the Yadavas, fought amongst themselves and killed each other. Lord Krishna and his brother Balarama were unable to stop them and watched helplessly as their sons and grandsons died before their eyes.

Lord Krishna, all alone and heartbroken, was sitting under a tree when the arrow of a hunter struck his ankle and he gave up his spirit and his soul rose to heaven. His city of Dwarka was then swallowed by Samudra, the Sea God.

In Indraprastha, Yudhishthira once again became the king and ruled with the help of his four brothers. Gandhari, Kunti, Vidura and Dhritarashtra left for the forest to live a simple life of prayer till their death.

When Arjuna's grandson and Abhimanyu's son Parikshit grew up, he was made to sit on the throne and the five Pandavas and Draupadi embarked on a pilgrimage to the Himalayas and walked towards Heaven, or Swarga.

The Pandavas and Draupadi lived as hermits. As they climbed higher and higher into the Himalayas praying for enlightenment, one by one they began to fall on the way.

Draupadi was the first to fall and before dying she asked Yudhishthira, "Why have I been stopped on my way to Swarga?" Yudhishthira explained, "Even though you were married to all five of us, you loved Arjuna the most."

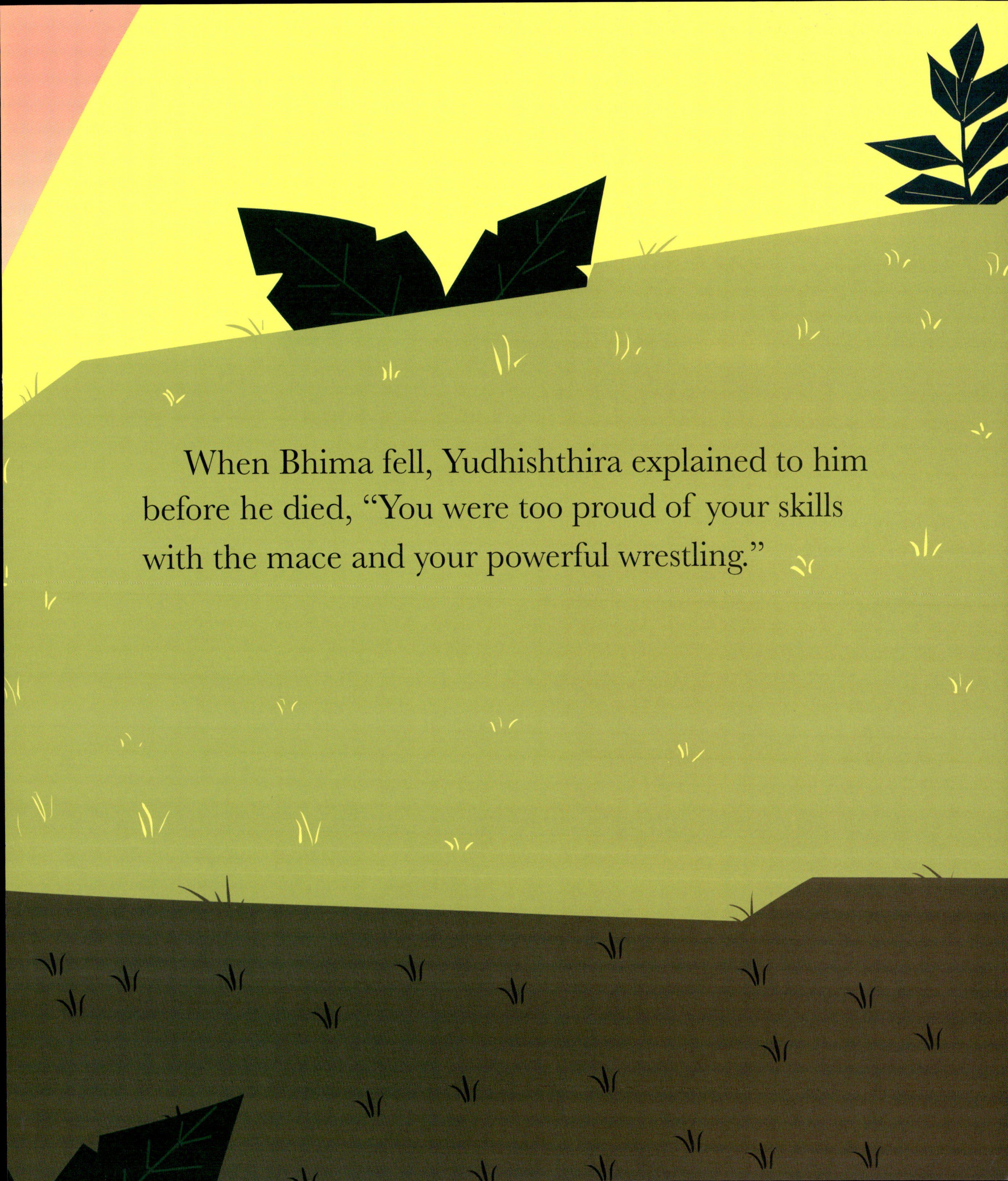

When Bhima fell, Yudhishthira explained to him before he died, “You were too proud of your skills with the mace and your powerful wrestling.”

When Arjuna collapsed on the mountain path, Yudhishthira told his brother, “You, Arjuna, were also too proud of your skills as a warrior and felt that no one could defeat you in archery. Your pride was your downfall.”

Nakul and Sahadev, explained Yudhishthira, were both vain about their good looks and their knowledge of the sacred books.

Now Yudhishthira climbed all alone towards Swarga through the snowy peaks and narrow, stony paths. He was accompanied by a dog who was, in fact, Dharmaraja Yama, the God of Death.

Yama explained to Yudhishthira that he would have to visit Naraka, the Underworld, because all rulers have to do that at least once. And when he is in Swarga, his wife and brothers will join him.

In Swarga, the five Pandava brothers and Draupadi were once again united with the Kauravas and all the men who had died in the great Battle of Kurukshetra. Finally, they all found peace and happiness together.